AIRPORTS, PORTS & LOGISTICS BEST PRACTICES DISCOVERIES

THE NARRATIVE ADAPTATION FROM THE QURAN

DR. NAZRY BIN YAHYA

PARTRIDGE

To order additional copies of this book, contact
Toll Free 800 101 2657 (Singapore)
Toll Free 1 800 81 7340 (Malaysia)
orders.singapore@partridgepublishing.com

www.partridgepublishing.com/singapore

CONTENTS

Iqrak

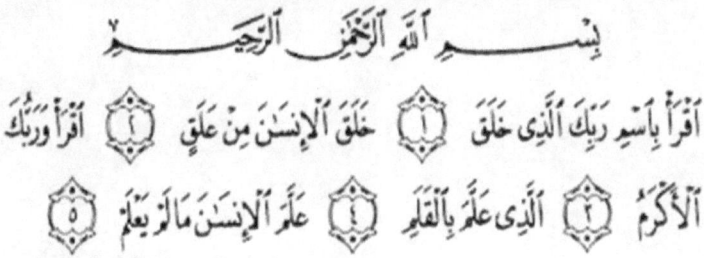

In the name of Allah, the most Gracious, the most Merciful

Read! In the Name of god, who has created (all that exist) [1].
Has created man from a clot [2].
Read! And your god is the Most Generous [3].
Who has taught (the writing) by the pen [4].
He has taught man that which he knew not [5].

Al-'Alaq 96:1-5

Preface

Alhamdullillah.

In the name of Allah, the Most Gracious, the Most Merciful

This book is finally completed despite the many challenges that I faced. I pray that all of us will find continuous Hidayah from Allah and get the Shafaat from Prophet Muhammad during the judgement day.

This book is not a book of Tafsir or the interpretation of the Quran. To learn Tafsir, you need to find a good Ustaz to guide you. This is the book about coining the narratives and the Ayats from the Quran in order to find the best practices for planning airports, ports and logistics operations.

This is a very handy book that can be read and understood at almost all level. All Quran references has been translated to English. For all the Arabic words that can't be translated, I have underlined it and you can refer it at the Glossary.

All of us should set a vision to be competent airports, ports and logistics professionals. Most importantly, let us all use this knowledge for us to become a better Muslim.

Dedication

To my mother and father.

To my wife.

To my children.

To my cats and fishes.

To the loving memories of the people who has left earlier.

To those who seeks the <u>Rahmat</u> from Allah…

Prelude

The Importance of Qasas or Narratives in the Quran

There is, in their stories, instruction for men endued with understanding. It is not a tale invented, but a confirmation of what went before it, a detailed exposition of all things, and a guide and a mercy to any such as believe.
Yusuf 12:111

The Quran is the revelation that Allah has given to Prophet Mohamad more than 1,400 years ago. The revelation comes in progressive manner to allow people to absorb its content.

One of the miracles of the Quran is that it can stand against time, industry, distance and across all races. Some 1,400 years ago, most of the Arabs were illiterate. But the Quran has remained the same as it was revealed to Prophet Muhamad without any changes until today.

The Quran has brought to the Arabs with the much-needed knowledge and people were then progressively able to build up a civilized community. It started from the Mekah and Madinah, and over the years it has become an Islamic Civilization.

There are 114 Surat with 6,236 Ayats in the Quran. If we break if down further, we will be able to digest the 1,000 Ayats that asks human being to do good deeds, 1,000 Ayats that prevents human being from doing bad deeds, 1,000 Ayats that spells about the torture in hell fire, 1,000 Ayats about comparison, 500 Ayats about Halal and Haram, 100 Ayats abouts prayers and praising Allah and 66 Ayats about Nasikh and Mansukh. And there are also 1,000 Ayats about news and stories.

Why is there 1,000 Ayats in the Quran that tells stories?

Small children always enjoy listening to stories. And storytelling is still an enjoyable tool that adults also cherishes. It's a dopamine that human being is seeking to enhance the learning capacity.

Listening to stories during childhood is definitely a pleasurable experience that the brain can experience. Continuous reading of good stories too enhances the memories and adaptation of the concepts that the author would like to convey. And this is the beauty of the Quran.

1,400 years ago, the Quran already has 1,000 Ayats that tells stories. Allah has created this to allow people back then and the future people to understand the same thing. Can you imagine the knowledge gaps back then and now? 1,400 years ago, not many people who were literate, but through stories they are able to grasp the knowledge, preach and practice it.

The Quran is presented in Arabic. Allah has also confirmed that the Quran is revealed in the simplest language for people to understand and to memorize. This is in line with Allah's words:

And We have certainly made the Qur'an easy for remembrance,
so is there any who will remember?

Qamar 54: 17

Reading and listening to stories is a pleasurable experience that the brain remembers and continues to seek throughout life. Strong emotional memory connections are intrinsic to the experiences of listening to stories. That is why the Quran tells the stories that people may not know and may not have the scientific knowledge. Please do understand that the knowledge gap of 1,400 years is not a small feat.

Anyone can learn or memorize anything they want. All it takes is repetition, practice, and most importantly- patience. There are millions of people who have memorized the Quran which consists of 77,430 words. And to have stories in the Quran makes is a lot simple. You just need to have a clear vision, a strong determination and practice.

This book also takes the approach to learn from the words of Allah and digest the lesson learned from the stories in the Quran. The stories or Qasas from the Quran is one of the tools to help readers to understand and to adapt. The narratives come in different forms and for different purposes. Some of the stories includes description of certain events, stories of the nations that was far away in terms of distance and time from the Mekah, stories of the prophets and many more.

Among others, the stories include names like the intelligent Luqman, the pure Maryam, the condemned Firaun, the prophets and many more. The objective of telling stories is very clear – it is a teaching methodology for people to understand, to adopt, to be able to memorize and to serve as a reminder and warner.

Today, via consistent researches psychologist has concluded that messages that's delivered as stories can be twenty-two (22) times more memorable than just facts. And the Quran already recognized this thousands of years ago and this is another miracle of the Quran.

What is it about narratives that promotes the understanding and easier memorization? Among others psychologist are able summarize into three facts: -

a) Stories engage our emotions

> The stories from <u>Surat</u> Luqman allows our inner fillings to have sympathy and to treat our children with wisdom. On the other hand, the stories of the Firaun, touches our emotions to stop doing unwanted things.

b) Stories act a "mnemonic devices for facts"

> The mnemonic works by organizing difficult material into meaningful division for easier learning. A good example is at <u>Surat</u> Ar-Rahman where Allah says:

The sun and the moon follow their measured-out calculation.
Ar-Rahman 17:5

In addition to that, Allah has repeatedly mentioned this verse:

Then which of the Blessings of your Lord
will you both [jinn and men] deny?
Ar-Rahman 17: *31 times*

c) Stories forces our self to use our brain differently

A recent research proves that our brain can develop a feeling of "being lost during reading or hearing stories that we hardly notice about the world around us. During this period, readers or listeners will be able to fit into the shoes of the protagonist to feel what they are feeling. That is why, some people cry when they read and understand the Quran.

Wallahualam!

CHAPTER 1

Introduction to Islamic Management Principles

There are 27 places in the Quran that mentions the word Ajaba. Ajaba can be translated as the miracle or wonderful.

Ajaba is the best description about the Quran. For those who reads, the Quran consists of all knowledge sets including life skills, human relations, quantum mechanics, Big Bang Theory, genetics, geology, thermodynamics, hydrogen fuel cells, strategic planning, procurement, logistics and many more. All the scientific theories are presented in the simplest language so that the people who read the Quran some 1,400 years ago can have considerable understanding with the knowledge of the people living now. The Quran also shows that the Ajaba can help human and Jins to experience peace. The words of the Quran too is comforting that it will allow us to become more motivated in our daily lives

Say: It has been revealed to me that a company of Jins listened (to the Qur'an). They said, 'We have really heard a wonderful Ajaba Recital!
Aj-Jin 72: 1

In another Ayat, Allah has reminded that we should feel thankful and obsessed with what god has given to us.

Or dost thou reflect that the Companions of the Cave and
of the Inscription were wonders among Our Sign?
Al-Kahfi 18: 9

The above Ayat too is a reminder to some people who feel at awe to some of the world's miracles but do not feel the importance to the words of Allah in the Quran.

All these while we have been fully exposed to the Western type of management principles. Thousands of books and journals has been produced by scholars and researchers. Unfortunately, we don't really see much attention given to Islamic management principles as was narrated from the Quran.

So, what is management? The popular definition is the process of administering and controlling the activities of the organization. It is an act of creating and maintaining such a business environment wherein the members of the organization can work together to achieve business objectives efficiently and effectively. Managers too have the core function of planning, leading, organizing and controlling. The other two core functions of a manager include staffing and motivating the staff.

The managers main tasks are to control and efficiently ensure the productivity and the quality of the 6Ms that is the Material, Money, Machine, Market, Method and Man.

Then what is Islamic management principles?

Islam is actually a way of life; thus, Islam is not just limited to the prayer mats and submission to Allah. Everything that we do must have Islam and Allah as our guidance. Our ultimate aim as a human being is to have the Redha from Allah and the ultimate success is to stay away from hell fire and to be rewarded with the Jannah.

Having said this, the main difference between Western Management Principle if compared to Islamic Management Principles is **Niat**. We need to set a good Niat in order to get the Redha from Allah. With a good Niat too, will prevent managers from doing bad things.

The other functions of Islamic Management Principles include factors like Niat, Planning, Execution, Organization, Leading, Controlling and Evaluation.

a) Niat

As explained earlier, Niat is the main difference in determining the existence of an Islamic management principle. This is because a sincere Niat to do great job will ensure that the program will be run according to allowable clauses in Islam. The Niat should always be towards the Redha of Allah

b) Planning

This is the same with the Western. The only difference is while in the course of doing business, if there are any Haram or Gharar activities, then it has to be stopped to ensure only permissible businesses are run.

3

c) Execution

Execution here means that the assigned job is done with the fullest Amanah. A true Islamic manager will work not just for profit, but to think of ways to make more money and eventually pay Zakat for the community. Towards the end, the Islamic managers introduces the concept of Tawakkal. This concept actually is an act of submission to Allah where once a person has done his or her job as best possible, then he or she will pray to Allah so that the job will be turned to be as planned.

d) Organization

This is the same with the Western principles. The only difference is in the course of doing business, if there are any Haram or Gharar activities, then it has to be stopped to ensure only Halal businesses are run. Flexibility too is appreciated as KPI is not the whole thing that Islamic Management requires.

e) Leading

This is the same with the Western. The only difference is in the course of doing business, if there are any Haram or Gharar activities, then it has to be stopped to ensure only permissible businesses are run. Leadership should always be by example.

f) Controlling

This is the same with the Western. The only difference is while in the course of doing business, if there are any Haram or Gharar activities, then it has to be stopped to ensure only permissible businesses are run. The concept of Amal Makruf Nahi Mungkar

4

too is applicable here to ensure that only good deeds are perform and no sins are presence. The Doa too is another critical element in Islamic principle because the Doa recital, it is when we are nearest to Allah.

g) Evaluation

This is another clear difference from the Western thought. Every airports, ports and logistics personals has to look into what he or she is doing on daily, weekly, monthly, quarterly and yearly basis. The evaluation is to ensure the management of the organization is run as efficiently possible.

Listed below is the four other Islamic evaluation methods to follow: -

i) **Musyaratah**

> We need to give our own self advices. There is no one else better to give advices except to own self. This is a difficult thing to do, but required to ensure integrity of the system is intact.

ii) **Muraqabah**

> To feel always attached to Allah by reeling that Allah watches what His creations are doing at all the time. We should only do allowable things that follows the rules of the Quran.

iii) Muhasabah

We should always on daily basis check if we have done better than the day before. The checks are on individual basis or organization basis.

O you who have believed, fear Allah. And let every soul look to what it has put forth for tomorrow - and fear Allah. Indeed, Allah is Acquainted with what you do
Al-Hashar 59:18

iv) Muaqabah

By punishing own self and to feel remorse if we have done something bad. It can be achieved after checking on Muhasabah. Taubat is the key element and managers should be thinking of not wanting to repeat the mistake again, ever!

In summary, **Table 1** below explains the difference between Western types of management if compared to Islamic management.

Western Management	Islamic Management
-	**Niat**
Planning	Planning
-	**Execution**
Organizing	Organizing
Leading	Leading
Controlling	Controlling
-	**Evaluation**

Table 1: *Difference between Western and Islamic Management*

The other two common principle of Islamic condition is: -

a) <u>Syura</u>. This means making decision based on meeting agreements. <u>Syura</u> always looks things as <u>Husnu Zon</u> (good thought or intentions).

b) Term of Reference is always the Quran and <u>Hadith</u>.

Wallahualam!

CHAPTER 2

Introduction to Logistics

In Islam, we need to define the allowable ways to transport goods from one place to another. Islamic practicing logistician should always think the best ways to ensure that the Islamic integrity is not compromised.

To further understand that, we will look back into the conventional principle of logistics. The logistics is normally analysed from its material management and its distribution network. This means that logistics comprises of all warehousing activities, from the trucking of the product (finished or semi-finished) to the end-customers.

One of the most commonly accepted definition of logistics is: *The process of planning, implementing and controlling the efficient, effective flow and storage of goods, services, and related information from point of origin to point of consumption for the purpose of conforming to customers' requirements*. This book shall follow the above definition as the basis to understand more about logistics.

The conventional logistics knowledge too acknowledges that one of the accepted keys performance indicator is when the logistician

is able to adhere the 7 R's or the 7 Rights of Logistics. The 7 R's are as shown in the **Figure 1** below:-

Figure 1: *The 7 R's of Logistics*

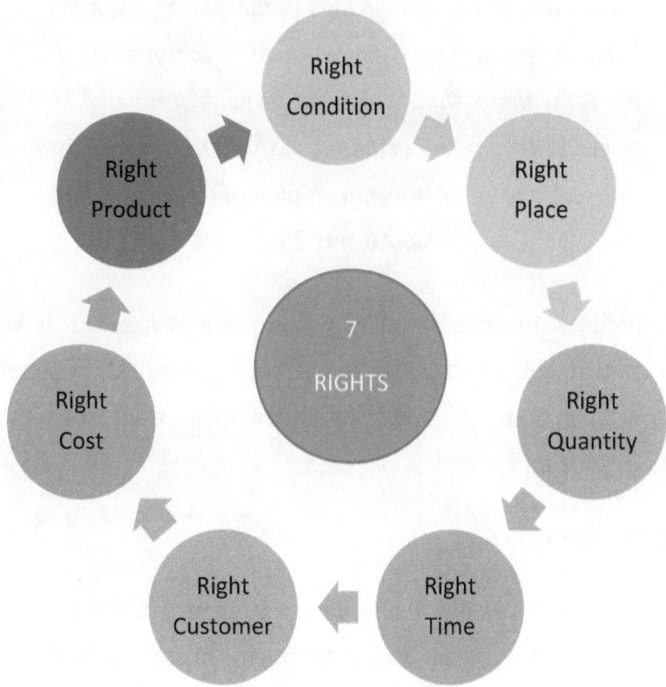

The 7 R's is in line with Allah's word that only accept the straight path or the non-compromised integrity.

> *"I put my trust in Allah, My Lord and your Lord! There is not a moving creature, but He hath grasp of its fore- lock. Verily, it is my Lord that is on a straight Path.*
> **Hud 11:56**

In Surat Az-Zumar, Allah further reminded people that all activities in the world will go through a cycle that is consistent

over time that He has predetermined. This is for people to continue to remember him.

> *Seest thou not that Allah sends down rain from the sky,*
> *and leads it through springs in the earth? Then He*
> *causes to grow, therewith, produce of various colours:*
> *then it withers; thou wilt see it grow yellow; then He*
> *makes it dry up and crumble away. Truly, in this, is a*
> *Message of remembrance to men of understanding*
> **Az-Zumar 39:21**

Let's try now to understand why this 7 R's of logistics is very important to the airports, ports and logistics world. Whenever there is movement of goods, logistics will be tracked by these seven basic elements.

a. Right condition:

The cargo must arrive at the destination in exactly the same condition that the buyer wants. Shippers must plan of the best method to ensure that the cargo expected delivery condition is achieved. For instance, in the case of cocoa bean exports via container, the shippers normally will add on desiccants to absorb excessive water.

b. Right place:

If the cargo is consigned to Thailand it should reach Thailand and not elsewhere. Reaching the wrong destination will trigger additional shipping costs. The buyer will insist that the seller to

be responsible for movement of the cargo to its right location. The buyer will not pay for the additional moving cost.

c. Right quantity:

If the order is to send 1,000 MT of 5% White Rice in 50 kg bags, then 1,000 MT of 5% White Rice in 50 kg bags must reach its destination. The buyer will demand the total quantity and quality to match the purchase order. If there are variations to the order, the seller will be responsible to replace at the seller's costs.

d. Right time:

Buyers normally give the window for the cargo to be delivered within a certain time period. Delivery must be made during the window period given. If the seller is unable to meet the delivery date, the buyer must be notified early. This is to prevent future disputes or being charged a penalty fee.

e. Right customer:

If XYZ Company orders the cargo, then only XYZ Company should receive the cargo. The delivery address should be clearly stated in the purchase order to ensure correct delivery instructions.

f. Right cost:

If the company agrees on the logistics cost of only USD10 per unit, then the supplies must be sent at the maximum of USD10 per unit. The price quoted in the terms for contract is for the completion of the whole job. Additional costs shall be borne by the seller. The costing is a very delicate issue in logistics.

g. Right product:

If the order is for oranges, then only oranges of the required grade shall reach the buyer's destination. A buyer will not agree to substitution of products as it will not comply with their own procurement, production or even sales requirements. Thus, the right product must be inspected and sent accordingly.

Fulfilling the 7 Rs in logistics is the key ingredient to all the concepts discussed in this book. It covers all aspects including supply chain management and Incoterms. It also proves the word of Allah in the Quran.

Wallahualam!

CHAPTER 3

Trading Practices

The utility concept and the value of goods are very closely related to each other. Goods are valueless unless they are transported to a new place which has demand. For example, Vietnam produces millions of tonnes of rice but the country only consumes a fraction of the rice produced. If the rice is not exported out of Vietnam, then there is no demand. It will reduce the price and possible quality degradation of the rice. However, international countries like the Philippines and Indonesia need the rice from Vietnam. This scenario created a *place utility* concept where the goods at the new place (in this case the Philippines and Indonesia) has more value than the rice if it is not sold in the original country (in this example Vietnam).

Another important utility concept to understand is *time utility*. This concept explains that certain goods are only important and has more value during certain limited time frame. For instance, during the weeks of the Chinese Lunar New Year, the demand for mandarin oranges is extremely high. But one month before and one month after the Chinese Lunar New Year, the mandarin oranges have become less important and less expensive.

The utility concept is the foundation of buying and selling locally and internationally. Some countries can continue to work on its best quality product and start the buy and sell. Historically the international trade can be traced back as early as 2,000 BCE when the tribes from Northern Africa traded dates and clothing with Babylonia and Assyria in the Middle East for spices and olive oil.

The logistics practices of local and international trading can be simple as long as buyers and sellers continue to observe what Allah has instructed in the Quran. There are many verses in the Quran where we can extract and use as our guide. Among other, the Quran reminds us to be very precise in our documentations. There should not be any wrongs in our documents.

a) Documentation

The Quran has no flaws. Some 1,400 years ago the Quran was first revealed to Prophet Muhammad SAW who was known to the Arabs as a trustworthy but ummi (illiterate man).

How can a man who was illiterate manage to memorize all the 6,236 Ayats in the Quran? Today, the Ayats are still exactly the same as when it was revealed to Prophet Muhammad.

In Surat Al Baqarah, Allah said

> *This is the Book about which there is no doubt,*
> *a guidance for those conscious of Allah*
> **Al-Baqarah 2:2**

According to Al-Syahid Hassan al-Banna, the Quran is a complete constitution that covers the whole Islamic principles. The Quran

too is the ultimate source that purifies the knowledge into the heart of those who seeks the Redha of Allah.

We have, without doubt, sent down the Message; and
We will assuredly guard it (from corruption)
Al-Hijr 15: 9

There should not be any doubts about the authenticity of the Quran.

There should be any doubts too on the authenticity and the correctness of all logistics documents that we are exposed to.

Airports, ports and logistics documents like the Bill of Lading, Airway Bill, invoice, packing list and others should be fool proof and correct one hundred percent. All the documents should be checked, and rechecked as many times possible to ensure the correctness and validity of the document.

The Murphy's law is applicable in this situation whereby it was quoted that "*things will go wrong in any given situation, if you give them a chance*" or more commonly, "*whatever can go wrong, will go wrong*". Thus, we have to ensure that all the documents are correct in the first place and continue to be intact from the point of document production to the last place where the documents are presented.

b) Credit Terms

Islam is a complete religion that covers all aspect of life. This include sharing people the best way of taking credit. In Surat Al-Baqarah, Allah has reminded people that when we take loans, we have to write it down.

O you who have believed, when you contract a debt
for a specified term, write it down. And let a scribe
write [it] between you in justice. Let no scribe refuse
to write as Allah has taught him. So let him write
and let the one who has the obligation dictate.
Al-Baqarah 2:282

Logically speaking, to write down debt and also to acknowledge the person who is giving the debt is a noble thing to do. This will also prevent possible disputes in the future. Writing down and keeping up with the payment plan will further allow both parties (borrower and lender) to better managed their cash flow.

The Quran also reminded us to be very careful with our data. We need also to be fully responsible to what we have contracted as Allah is very detail.

To Allah belongeth all that is in the heavens and on
earth. Whether ye show what is in your minds or
conceal it, Allah Calleth you to account for it. He
forgiveth whom He pleaseth, and punisheth whom He
pleaseth, for Allah hath power over all things
Al-Baqarah 2:284

c) Cargo Insurance

Insurance is now an integral part of modern business. Billions of US dollars in premium was paid to provide all kinds of protection. Yet, the same number of dollars was paid yearly to settle claims for incidences, catastrophes and accidents.

Insurance management has been structurally practised by the Chinese and the Babylonian traders as early as 100 BCE. The Babylonians for instance, has developed the famous system, the Code of Hammurabi. This system worked in a similar manner as the current insurance system.

Years ago in order to hedge their position, the Chinese merchants redistributed their merchandise in few ships to cap possible loss due to any single ship capsizing when travelling along treacherous river rapids. The Chinese were wise by not putting all their eggs in one basket.

The main objective of businesses taking insurance is to hedge against possible losses. In Islam, the concept is further elaborated as the fortunate group of people is encouraged to help the unfortunate group of people. The Quran has clearly stated that Allah encourages human being to help each other.

O ye who believe! Violate not the sanctity of the symbols of Allah, nor of the sacred month, nor of the animals brought for sacrifice, nor the garlands that mark out such animals, nor the people resorting to the sacred house, seeking of the bounty and good pleasure of their Lord. But when ye are clear of the sacred precincts and of pilgrim garb, ye may hunt and let not the hatred of some people in (once) shutting you out of the Sacred Mosque lead you to transgression (and hostility on your part). Help ye one another in righteousness and piety, but help ye not one another in sin and rancour: fear Allah. for Allah is strict in punishment.

Al-Maidah 5:2

d) Moral

Good moral is a critical element to become a great airports, ports and logistics man. This is the foundation of being able to be trusted and bestowed with the much-needed responsibility.

Prophet Muhamad, before he was appointed as a prophet was a very successful trader. He was known to be *Al Amin*, a tittle given to him by the Arabs to be the trustworthy one.

> *Verily, Allah commands that you should render back*
> *Amanah to those, to whom they are due; and that when*
> *you judge between men, you judge with justice.*
> **An-Nisa 4:58**

The airports, ports and logistics world are a dynamic yet highly regulated industry. That is why there are two main phrases that is constantly being discussed that is "Key Performance Indicators" and "Standard Operating Procedure". Anywhere that you go, you will always hear these 2 phrases being discuss in length.

The importance of possessing a good moral has been mentioned many times in the Quran. The word Amanah has been mentioned 20 times in the Quran in many Surats. The Amanah is only applicable to humans and Jin, while other entities like animals will not possess this quality.

Today, we can see that many airports, ports and logistics people who may not take the Amanah or the responsibility in the manner it should be taken. The inability to accept and honour given the

Amanah is not acceptable. Amanah should be the core values and highest priority in all airports, ports and logistics people.

In a Hadith that is recorded by Al-Bukahri and Muslim: -

> *Prophet Muhamad SAW said that there are three signs of a*
> *hypocrite – when he speaks, he lies; when he makes promise,*
> *he breaks it; when he is trusted, he betray the trust*

Amanah is all about fulfilling your obligations in the best possible manner. If any airports, ports or logistics officers is unable to fulfil his or her responsibilities, it is a sign of mistrust and deception. Allah has promised that on Day of Judgment, all dishonest people will be given the punishment that is equivalent to the breach of trust that they were given.

Amanah does have a very beautiful meaning. Thus, we need to push forward the importance of fulfilling it. If any airports, ports and logistics people betray the trust given to them, the impact will be very costly to the organization. Amanah too is the trust Allah SWT places in you to make the better judgements. In Surat Al-Anfal, Ayat No.27, Allah said: -

> *O you who have believed, do not betray Allah*
> *and the Messenger or betray your trusts*
> *while you know the consequence.*
> **Al-Anfal 8:27**

Allah has repeatedly reminded us to ensure Amanah is kept to the highest level. For example: -

And they who are to their trusts and their promises attentive
Al-Mukminum 23:8

Indeed, we offered the Trust to the heavens and the earth and the mountains, and they declined to bear it and feared it; but man [undertook to] bear it. Indeed, he was unjust and ignoran
Al-Ahzab 33:72

Amanah is a huge responsibility that not all Allah's creation is willing to take it; except human being. As mentioned in Surat Al-Ahzab Ayat No. 72, it shows how unjust and ignorant of human being to accept such huge tasks. Accepting the Amanah is one thing, but fulfilling the Amanah is where many human beings fails

Mentioned above is just four out of twenty Ayats that talks about Amanah in Islam. Its huge responsibility and not many of us can fulfil it. Just like work too. Once we are given the Amanah, we have to ensure that our works is one of the best produced which comply with the KPI and SOP that has been agreed before.

e) Truthful

The Quran is a very special book that is not comparable to others. The content of the Quran is relevant across time and culture. Dr. Yusof Al-Qaradhawi in one of his comments asked "How can we interact with the Quran?". Among others he quoted from Surat Hud.

> *Alif, Laam, Raa'. (This is) a Book, with verses basic or fundamental of established meaning),*

further explained in detail, from One Who is
Wise and Well-acquainted (with all things)
Hud 11:1

Airports, ports and logistics officers must always be prepared to get things done in the best possible manner. The Quran is a book of truth, thus the product of the people working in the industry too must be truthful to ensure the longevity and the integrity of the system stays intact.

Since Quran is the book of truth, we like to conclude that all the documents that goes around with the movement of goods too should be 100% correct. There is no way that we can accept documents that is half correct or documents that have flaws. All logisticians should be aware that mixing correct documents with false document will make the document invalid. We should uphold the integrity and the correctness of all document.

Wallahualam!

CHAPTER 4

Best Practices in Logistics
Adapted from the Quran

Best practices are the commonly observed programs that will allow organizations to achieve it best performance. The best practice is applicable to both profit oriented and non-profit oriented organizations.

We can read many of these examples in the stories that are told in the Quran. To match the requirement of airports, ports and logistics, we have divided the best practises into several areas as shown below: -

   a. Strategic Planning
   b. Time management
   c. Demand planning
   d. Logistics planning
   e. Warehousing
   f. Transportation
   g. Unit Load Devices
   h. Accounting & Bookkeeping

a)   Strategic Planning

When we discuss about strategic planning, it always starts with the end in mind. A strategist will know what the outcome will look like, before he or she starts to work on a project. It always starts with a "VISION" of the end.

The Quran shares a story about the Prophet Yusof as one of the examples of best practice. This story too will be shared again in Chapter 5 on Risk Management. From Ayat 46-49, the Quran recites the story when Prophet Yusof is still being imprisoned for a theft that he did not commit.

The ruling King of Egypt at that time had recurring dreams about 7 fat cows being eaten by 7 skinny cows. Later, the King continues to dream about 7 green wheat and the other 7 dry wheat. He was looking for an interpreter of his dream but couldn't find one.

Yusof, O man of truth, explain to us about seven fat cows eaten by seven [that were] lean, and seven green spikes [of grain] and others [that were] dry - that I may return to the people; perhaps they will know [about you]."

Yusof said, "You will plant for seven years consecutively; and what you harvest leave in its spikes, except a little from which you will eat.

Then will come after that seven difficult [years] which will consume what you saved for them, except a little from which you will store

23

Then will come after that a year in which the people will be given rain and in which they will press [olives and grapes].

Yusof 12:46-49

The only one person that is able to interpret is Prophet Yusof. So, the King messenger went to the prison and met with Prophet Yusof. The dream interpretation is to be shared to the King and for the benefit of the country as the whole. Prophet Yusof clearly define the dream with full vision.

According to Prophet Yusof, the country will experience the next 7 years of prosperity. The prosperity is not to be misused, as the following 7 years the country will then experience severe drought. The seeds of the first 7 years will have to be saved for survival. Finally, Prophet Yusof said that only on the 15th year, then only the situation will return as normal.

Analysing this, the Qasas shares a story of how we should plan ahead for all our resources. Today it has been proven that most economic cycles have about 7 to 10 years gestation period. Prophet Yusof, knows what he wants in 7 years and the next 7 years. Prophet Yusof too knows that only in the 15th year the plants will be back as normal.

Proper vision need to be applied while planning for airports, ports and logistics operations and managing of resources. We just can't just spend now and hope that the future is bright. We need to plan the whole flow including manpower, time, resources, money and

also other things that we seldom forget like the usage of utilities like water and electricity.

Having a vision ahead will allow logisticians to estimate the cost and possible profit. This will further allow companies to operate more efficiently and effectively.

b) Time management

Islam has reminded us to be really cautious about time. There are 5 things that we need to adhere and understand. From Ibnu Abas, Prophet Muhamad SAW has reminded us 5 things before the coming of the 5 things: -

- Young before we become old
- Healthy before we become sick
- Rich before we become pauper
- Free time before we become busy; and
- Living before we die

This Hadith is actually a good reminder to all of us that we need to plan our time ahead of everything. In Islam, there is no procrastination. What need to be done now, must be done now. In Islam too there is no such thing as free time, we need to continuously make our self busy with zikir and praising Allah at all time. We should nor waste any money.

In Surat Al-Asr the Quran has stated in 3 very short Ayats, but has the longest interpretation and Tafsir.

In the name of time
Indeed, human being are in the state of pauperness

Except for those who have believed and done
righteous deeds and advised each other to truth
and advised each other to patience.

Al-Asr 1-3

Ibnu Taimiyyah RA had interpreted that there are two things that will prevent human being to have a true submission to Allah. The two are: -

- Shubuhaat – doubt
- Shahawaat – the evil passion

The first 2 Ayats of this Surat mentioned that human being is in the state of pauperness, unless he or she fulfils Ayat 3 which clearly clarify what need to be done.

Ayat 3 of this Surat, is able to eliminate the Shubuhaat by the continuously reminding people towards the truth. This will allow people to realize which is the truth and which is not. Moreover, the end of the Ayat 3 said, to give advices with patients actually is the key to defy Shahawaat from dominating the person. The ability to control the Shubuhaat and Shahawaat will allow people to gain the long-lasting paradise that has been promised by god in the Quran.

In the perspective of airport, port and logistics practices, we are reminded on few major things: -

I.   The need to put Allah ahead in all task

a. Most of us has put too much emphasize on work. We tend to forget that the main reason why we have to work is because of <u>Lillahi Taala</u>. We work because of Allah.

b. Due to that, most of us forgot the main duties of a worker that is to comply to <u>Solat</u> requirement, the <u>Zakat</u> obligation, the need to be fair to everyone and others.

c. Work has become too regimented that the workers is not able to practice the requirement of a Muslim.

d. As a worker, if we obey the command of God, we can assure the he or she will work as best possible to get the <u>Redha</u> from Allah, and of course the <u>Rezeki</u> that comes with the work.

II. The need to plan ahead

a. The best work that will be produced is the work that has been planned ahead.

b. There is no such thing in airports, ports and logistics dictionary where planning has never occurred.

c. The whole team need to have regular discussions internally and with their customers to chart the planning direction.

d. Everything need to be check and planned including: -

   i.   Man
   ii. Machine
   iii. Money

    iv. Market

    v. Material

    vi. Method

    vii. Safety

III. The job of a supervisor, manager and head of departments

a. While some people are doing the job, there must be some other people checking the process and the results.

b. There must be a check and balance in the activities, and the best person to identify it is the immediate supervisors, managers and also the head of departments

c. The job of an Islamic manager need to be complied at all time

    i. Niat

    ii. Planning

    iii. Execution

    iv. Organizing

    v. Leading

    vi. Controlling

    vii. Evaluation

d. The rest of the team members too need to support by being a reliable leader to ensure that the objectives are being met.

IV. The need to be patience in doing delicate things

a. The Quran has mention about being patience. That is precisely the thing that need to be done

       and the criteria that is required of a good Muslim logistician.

b. For instance, in the case of doing a warehouse stock count. There will be one thousand and one things to be counted. No items should not be left unaccounted. Stock count is one of the most stressful activity that a warehouseman would experience, especially when the warehousemen are unable to locate any stocks. Any act of being impatience will possibly make the stock count as inconclusive.

c) Demand planning

In today's world, supply chain dependency on system application has become very important. Sometimes jobs are put on hold when the system is down. There are three main components in demand planning that is production planning, logistics demand planning and sales and operations integration planning. Why do we need all these?

To forecast accurately is tough. Forecasts can be 100% correct or 100% wrong. Demand planning will require the most accurate forecast possible; and this is the toughest part for all organizations. The forecast can be in the form of daily, weekly, monthly or even yearly production forecast. The demand planning actually rationalizes the details in logistics planning. Thus, an organization must be able to look into cumulative logistics costing and maximize its potentials.

The Quran is the documentary proof of the messenger hood of the Prophet Muhammad; while the raw materials consists of letters and words that was revealed over a period of twenty-three years in accordance with the particular needs that emerged over time. The revelation in twenty-three years actually provide the guidance to the Prophet and his Sahabats step by step toward their exalted goals.

The Quran possess new language style that is neither poetic nor instructional. The expressions of the Quran are harmonious and its words are set together pleasingly and with the utmost beauty. The unique combination of wording and meaning is a special feature of the Quran and another aspect of its miraculousness.

I) Production Planning

Production planning refers to the production teams' readiness to proceed with a job. It is closely related to demand planning whereby accurate forecasting is the key component. Parties involved in production planning are normally the production manager, technical manager and the operators.

Effective production planning will result in lower production costs and better product quality. For instance, with better production planning, raw material purchases can be delayed and finished products will be directly sent to customers. Therefore, no storage cost is involved.

II) Logistics Demand Planning

Companies must look for ways to reduce wastage. Effective logistics demand planning will ensure minimum wastage in the organization. Coordination is important to allow minimum

trucking movement, minimum storage days but maximum capacity allowed for movement.

The best product handling is when there is no handling at all. We also explained that the best storage is when we are able to perform just-in-time (JIT) production, whereby the raw material goes straight to the production line from the vendors. In this case, the raw material has avoided double handling of being received and stored in the warehouse. Logistics planning will assist in reducing operating costs.

III) Sales and Operations Integration Planning

The sales and operations team must work closely to meet the optimum production capacity. The sales and operations team often struggle to meet the expectation of demanding customers. An operations team having to work overtime in order to meet the delivery schedule is not unheard of. But by working overtime, the organization has reduced its profitability as there are additional costs involved that have not been planned or budgeted for.

The sales and operations team need to find a balance in order to maximize the company's profitability. There is a mismatch of needs from the operations and the sales perspective. A good example is when the operations team want longer lead time if compared to the shorter lead time required by the sales team. A shorter lead time will force the operations team to work harder, incurring higher costs to pay for overtime, machine maintenance and others.

The operations team would prefer to have a stable schedule while the sales team would require a variable schedule. A variable

schedule for the sales team allows for a variety of orders to be delivered upon customer order confirmation. Therefore, it is very important for the sales and operations team to strike a balance in their workload to better manage service and delivery.

d)   Logistics planning

Logistics planning involves all the factors related to logistics such as warehouse, forwarding and transportation, which include freighting, trucking and rail. All the activities must fulfill the 7 Rs of logistics. (Details of the logistics activities were presented in Chapter 2)

As detail out in Surat Al-Baqarah: -

> *The lightning all but snatches away their sight; every time the light (Helps) them, they walk therein, and when the darkness grows on them, they stand still. And if Allah willed, He could take away their faculty of hearing and seeing; for Allah hath power over all things.*
> **Al-Baqarah 2: 20**

> ***Note:*** *Direct translation for lightning is Buraq, the vehicle that Prophet Muhamad uses during his journey. The Buraq is an animal that is slightly bigger than a donkey and smaller than a horse. Some say that the Buraq is a white horse with wings. Some other say that the Buraq is a big white bird. Wallahualam!*

This Ayat is an example of how the Buraq travels to assist Prophet Muhammad SAW during his journey during the Israq and Mikraj. Israq is actually the journey from Masjidil Haram to

Masjidil Aqsa while Mikraj is the Prophet's journey across seven skies while meeting the earlier prophets (Adam, John, Jesus, Yusof, Enoch, Aaron, Moses, Abraham), witnessing the hell and paradise and finally stops at the Sidratul Muntaha. This is the time too when Prophet Muhamad got the instructions to carry out the mandatory prayers five times per day. The knowledge gained was abundant, but Prophet Muhamad was able to journey all the long distance all through the night.

An effective logistics plan will assist officers in managing last minute disruptions and to prevent mishaps. This will also involve communication skills and the ability to find alternative solutions for immediate execution.

In addition to that, a great logistician too needs to look into production planning. This is the process to find the efficiency level for procurement, purchase, acceptance of raw material and production. This includes managing the inventory level and triggering the purchase alert whenever raw material has reached safety stock levels.

Another important element in logistics planning is also about workforce planning. Workforce planning refers to the human resources needs for production. The workforce may include permanent staff, temporary staff and even contractors. For permanent and temporary staff, the human resources department of the organization would need to prepare employment letters or contracts for services respectively. However, for contractors, the procurement department would need to prepare contracts which include items like job scope, rate, liquidated ascertain damage

and other requirements deemed necessary, such as compliance to personal protective equipment, ISO and others.

Workforce planning also includes maintaining control and visibility of employees under the organization. Managers should be able to calculate effects of delays and unexpected events. When dealing with human beings, we are often exposed to unexpected events such as staff falling sick and coming in late to work due to emergencies. All these delays need to be factored into the plan and alternative solutions need to be made clear, such as having suitable replacement staff whenever possible.

e) Warehousing

All warehouses have three basic functions: movement, storage and information transfer. Interestingly, as the supply chain concept evolution reaches maturity, more emphasis has been given to the movement concept as most organizations look forward for better inventory turnover and faster delivery to final destinations.

I) Movement
Under movement, we can further elaborate the activities to five smaller elements to understand the function:

Receiving: The act of receiving cargo from an assigned transporter will involve the unloading of products from the carrier, inspection of cargo or damages, recordkeeping and also tally assignment. The standard receiving documents normally practiced are delivery order, invoice, packing list and tally sheet. Theoretically, the best type of receiving is not to receive the

cargo. This can be achieved if the cargo is directed to its final destination instead of coming into the warehouse first.

Put-away or transfer: This refers to the act of moving the received cargo to an assigned location in a warehouse for storage. You can also transfer the goods to a specific area for value-added warehouse activities. Three normal put-away activities are:

i)   Direct put-away—staging and inspecting activities are eliminated;
ii) Directed put-away—the warehouse management system shall give directions for where to place the cargo, and
iii) Batched or sequenced put-away—normally placed in zones and later put into slots/locations.

Order picking or cargo selections: This refers to the act of locating the cargo, sorting and then sending for shipping based on the customer's instructions. Order picking is put-away in reverse. A generally accepted distribution standard of an order picker's working time is as follows:

i)   Travelling – 55%;
ii) Searching – 15%;
iii) Extracting – 10%; and
iv) Others – 20%.

Unfortunately, due to inefficiency in many areas, most warehouse operators normally use 55% per cent of their time to search for the cargo. This is way beyond the internationally accepted distribution standard and causes time, space and fuel wastages

II) Storage

This second function of warehousing can be performed on a temporary basis or even a semi-permanent basis. The length of stay for each cargo shall depend more on the logistics system and the customer's demands. There are three commonly used methods to decide storage of goods.

Fixed locations: This is for regular stocked items with fixed addresses of goods locations. The cargo can easily be traced by the warehouse staff and could be expensive in terms of space commitments. The location must have sufficient room to accommodate additional stock.

Random locations: The cargo is put everywhere without proper planning. This is normally true for big engineering cargo such as ISO tanks, steel pipes or even ship spare-parts.

Zoning: Zone cargo is separated by the zones each cargo is categorize on the material zones for easy put away and order picking.

One of the most common questions that we get is how to get the information correct? We will explain this further in **Part (h) Accounting & Bookkeeping** of this chapter. As a heads up, the Quran explains that everything that god created is in pairs. But what do we mean by in pair?

We often hear that cancer has no cure. You can go for the chemotherapy treatment not to cured, but to reduce the exposure to of illness. But that is not true. The Quran said 23 times that everything is created in pair. Man vs Women. Heaven vs Hell.

Life vs Death. And many more. And this include sickness vs healing. Insyaallah there is a cure for cancer but we have not been exposed to that.

> *And of every thing We have created pairs: That*
> *ye may receive instruction to Glorify Allah*
> **Adz-Dzaariyaat 51:49**

> *That has created pairs in all things, and has made*
> *for you ships and cattle on which ye ride,*
> **Az-Zukhruf 43:12**

III) Information Transfer

The third major function of a warehouse is to provide accurate information transfer. Management and even customers, need fast and accurate inventory information as it attempts to administer and enhance warehouse operations.

Prophet Mohammad also said, in his Hadith as narrated by Abu Daud RA

> *Allah has sent down both the disease and the*
> *cure, and He has appointed a cure for every*
> *disease, so treat yourselves medically,*
> *but use nothing unlawful.*

The Quran has no flaws, right from the beginning until the final Ayat has been completed. God also challenges people who doubt the authenticities of the Quran to produce one Surat like it. To date, nobody dares and ever come close as the Quran is full of

true stories, scientific knowledge, medicine and it is comforting to the soul.

> *Oh people, if you doubt the heavenly origin of this*
> *Book which We have sent down to Our servant,*
> *the Prophet, produce one <u>Surat</u> like it.*
> **Al-Baqarah 2:23**

Principles of Material Handling while in storage

In managing the warehouse, all handlers should understand the basic principles of handling cargo. There are six basic principles to adhere to.

I) Safety principle
Safety is everything. Stretching and stooping are to be avoided.

II) Planning principle
All material movements need to be planned. Meetings need to be organized so that everyone is aware of the plan.

III) Simplification principle
You need to find ways to simplify the process. Think of ways to reduce, combine or eliminate a process. The least handled is the best handled. Handling increases cost, with minimum 15% but up to 80% of final cost.

IV) Gravity principle
This principle says that we must find ways to manage gravity. For example: -

    i)   Use rollers whenever possible.

ii) Push is much easier than pull.

iii) Two men handling the job is better than one.

V) Space utilization principle

Find ways to optimize the warehouse space as much possible because space costs money.

VI) Equipment selection principle

Need to use the correct equipment to handle each good. Mechanize whenever possible, rather than using physical manpower. Use gravity when moving goods instead of muscle.

VII) Principle of unit size

Handle loads in unit form. Standardized loads save time in receiving, storing, checking, etc. Also, the Quran has reminded us many times on segregation between Halal and Haram. We can't mix Halal and Haram cargoes and act together in one process. For example, the warehouse can't store books and liquor together. There must be a clear guideline which product can be handle and which are not allowed. In the case of food-based cargo, we also can't mix together Halal food and Non-halal produce in the same containment. That is not acceptable.

And do not eat up your property among yourselves for vanities, nor use it as bait for the judges, with intent that ye may eat up wrongfully and knowingly a little of (other) people's property.
Al-Baqarah 2:188

Prophet Mohammad SAW said:

Verily, the lawful is clear and the unlawful is clear, and between the two of them are doubtful matters about which many people do not know. Thus, he who avoids doubtful matters clears himself in regard to his religion and his honour, and he who falls into doubtful matters will fall into the unlawful as the shepherd who pastures near a sanctuary, all but grazing therein. Verily, every king has a sanctum and the sanctum of Allah is his prohibitions. Verily, in the body is a piece of flesh which, if sound, the entire body is sound, and if corrupt, the entire body is corrupt. Truly, it is the heart.

Sahih Bukhari 52 & Sahih Muslim 1599

Prohibited to you are dead animals, blood, the flesh of swine, and that which has been dedicated to other than Allah, and [those animals] killed by strangling or by a violent blow or by a head-long fall or by the goring of horns, and those from which a wild animal has eaten, except what you [are able to] slaughter [before its death], and those which are sacrificed on stone altars, and [prohibited is] that you seek decision through divining arrows. That is grave disobedience. This day those who disbelieve have despaired of [defeating] your religion; so fear them not, but fear Me. This day I have perfected for you your religion and completed My favour upon you and have approved for you Islam as religion. But whoever is forced by severe hunger with no inclination to sin - then indeed, Allah is Forgiving and Merciful

Al-Maidah 5:3

The above verse explains the food item which are forbidden to Muslims to eat. However, there are exceptions to those who are dying from hunger. This group of people are allowed to eat whatever they find available to feed their hunger because Allah is the most merciful yet forgiving.

Other than edible things, Quran has also mentioned the non-edible things which are Haram. In Surat Al-Araf, Ayat number 33: -

My Lord has only forbidden immoralities - what is apparent of them and what is concealed - and sin, and oppression without right, and that you associate with Allah that for which He has not sent down authority, and that you say about Allah that which you do not know
Al-Araf 7:33

In the above verse Allah has declared the deeds which are Haram and why we should shy away from it. Islam is not only a religion but it is also the proper way of living, based on certain rules and regulations. So, in order to make our standards of living good and as per to the teachings of Islam, we should avoid committing deeds which are forbidden by the Lord.

Inventory management

Inventory management is the other element of the warehouse function. It is highly related because as soon as the cargo comes into the warehouse, the inventory process begins.

What is inventory? It simply means the quantity of goods held in a specified location at specific time in an unproductive state, waiting to be used or sold.

The following three are other inventory definitions that are important.

I) Inventory control
Inventory control is the technique of maintaining stock items at a predetermined desired level.

II) Inventory management
Inventory management is determining the policies that set the goals for the inventory control system.

III) Inventory policy
This is a statement of the company's goals and approach to the management of inventories. It normally comprises guidelines with regards (but not limited) to:

    i)   What to produce/procure;
    ii) What to sell/to stock;
    iii) In what quantities, and
    iv) When to take the appropriate action.

Practical Guide to Inventory Accuracy

Accurate inventory is at the heart of all warehouse operations. The fundamentals to achieve accuracy are as followings: -

I) Attitude.
All warehouse staff must have the correct attitude to carry out duties responsibly, and to work ethically and efficiently. Staff

must ensure that the cargo is treated with proper care and concern. This is in line with the Ayat in the Quran which teaches us to have great attitude and be nice to human being, animals and to mother nature.

Allah forbids you not, with regard to those who fight you not for (your) Faith nor drive you out of your homes, from dealing kindly and justly with them: for Allah loveth those who are just.

Al-Mumtahanah 60:8

II) Process or procedure definition

All processes or business procedures need to be defined and charted. When the Quran was revealed to Prophet Muhammad, it was from Angel Jibril to Prophet Muhammad verbally. Then Prophet Muhammad teaches the Quran to his Sahabats. Over time we have many of the Sahabats who became Huffaz.

During those days, papers was not readily available to the Arabs. Prophet Muhammad with his wisdom requested that the Ayats to be written wherever possible on the rocks, animal skins and camel's bones. The whole process to create a written Quran in a proper book format was only completed 19 years after the passing of Prophet Muhammad. Nevertheless, the record keeping is accurate and the Quran that you read now is the same like one recited by Prophet Muhammad

III) Employee testing

Put new employees on a trial basis or on probation. This is to prevent sudden departure of new staff and allow them to adhere

to the agreed operations standards. All warehouse operators need to set a minimum standard. The best way is to look into the best industry practices, and apply it.

> *And be steadfast in patience; for verily Allah will*
> *not suffer the reward of the righteous to perish.*

Hud 11:115

IV) Stock checking

Do not stop counting stock. Only physical counting can confirm the system's accuracy. One of the best Qasas from the Quran is the Ayat that explains that Prophet Sulaiman actually counts all his armies which consist of Jins, men and birds.

> *And before Solomon were marshalled his hosts- of Jins and*
> *men and birds, and they were all kept in order and ranks.*
> **An-Naml 27:17**

After that, the Quran eventually reveals that Prophet Sulaiman checks his army inventory and could not see his hoopoe (a type of bird). Be fully informed that Prophet Sulaiman has a big army, and yet he is able to count each of them and eventually discover that he is missing one bird.

> *And he took a muster of the Birds; and he said: "Why is*
> *it I see not the Hoopoe? Or is he among the absentees?*
> **An-Naml 27: 20**

Apart from practical guides explained above and also the stories that is shared, all warehouse operators should also look into

additional contributing factors such as dedicating core personnel for managing inventory. There should also be a mechanism to control employee turnover and encourage loyalty among staff members.

Warehouse managers should also be prepared to dismiss or re-assign employees as and when deemed as fit. There should be proper work ethics, guidelines and regular checks in place to prevent inappropriate handling of goods. To have accurate inventory, cargo must be stored at proper storage places.

f)   Transportation

For transportation, we will look the Qasas from the perspective of moving vehicles on sea, land and air. These are the three most common mode that we can learn.

The most important is to plan ahead. As explained earlier, we need to have a vision of the ending before we start. A good example is about performing Hajj. In Surat Al-Haj Ayat 27, the Quran mentioned that that Hajj is Wajib and all man (and women) will come to do their Hajj if they are capable and have extra resources.

And proclaim the Pilgrimage among men: they
will come to thee on foot and (mounted) on every
kind of camel, lean on account of journeys through
deep and distant mountain highways;
Al-Hajj 22:27

I) Shipping

Maritime or sea transport is essential to the world's economy as over 90% of the world's trade is carried by sea. It is by far, the most cost-effective way to move goods and raw materials around the globe. The sea uses the natural way thus able to save millions of dollars in building the required facilities.

Sea based transportation has a key role to play in the alleviation of extreme poverty and hunger as it already provides an important source of income and employment for many developing countries, such as the supply of seagoing personnel, ship recycling, ship owning, ship chartering, ship building, ship repair and related port services.

There is no wonder why Allah has mentioned the ease of shipping 16 times in the Quran. The followings are some of the Ayats from various Surats: -

And His are the Ships sailing smoothly
through the seas, lofty as mountains:
Ar-Rahmaan 55:24

It is Allah Who hath created the heavens and the earth and
sendeth down rain from the skies, and with it bringeth out
fruits wherewith to feed you; it is He Who hath made the
ships subject to you, that they may sail through the sea by His
command; and the rivers (also) hath He made subject to you.
Ibrahim 14:32

Behold! in the creation of the heavens and the earth; in the alternation of the night and the day; in the sailing of the ships through the ocean for the profit of mankind; in the rain which Allah Sends down from the skies, and the life which He gives therewith to an earth that is dead; in the beasts of all kinds that He scatters through the earth; in the change of the winds, and the clouds which they Trail like their slaves between the sky and the earth;- (Here) indeed are Signs for a people that are wise.
Al-Baqarah 2:164

And there are (other) advantages in them for you (besides); that ye may through them attain to any need (there may be) in your hearts; and on them and on ships ye are carried.
Ghaafir 40:80

The sea way is by far the cheapest and the most convenient mode of transportation. Allah too has promised to make the ships easy to handle at his command for our uses. From the traditional east to west pass, west to east pass, and more recently northwest passage, transpolar sea routes, artic bridge etc, the ships are freely to move across the globe.

Among His Signs is this, that He sends the Winds, as heralds of Glad Tidings, giving you a taste of His (Grace and) Mercy,- that the ships may sail (majestically) by His Command and that ye may seek of His Bounty: in order that ye may be grateful.
Ar-Ruum 30:46

It is Allah Who hath created the heavens and the earth and sendeth down rain from the skies, and with it bringeth out

fruits wherewith to feed you; it is He Who hath made the
ships subject to you, that they may sail through the sea by His
command; and the rivers (also) hath He made subject to you.
Ibrahim 14:32

II) Land Transportation

Today, we have many travellers who love to travel. In fact, we
hardly find anyone who doesn't want to travel to see the world.
Historically, we have seen many Muslim names who are known
for their famous travels. Among other the name Ibnu Batuta stands
ahead. Ibnu Batuta started his journey at the age of 20 years old to
fulfil the 5th pillar of Islam that is to perform the Hajj in Mekah.
Little did he foresee that his traveling went on for approximately
30 years and covered more than 120,000 kilometres visiting the
equivalent of 44 modern countries which were then mostly under
the governments of Muslim leaders of the World.

The other big Muslim name in travel is the Admiral Zheng Hee.
Unlike Ibnu Batuta, Admiral Zheng Hee travels by using the sea
route in China, South East Asia, India, Arab states and also to
some parts of Africa.

There are 9 Ayats in the Quran that mentions about the importance
to prepare for a journey. If we travel and able to observe God's
greatness, the journey will also bring Pahala. That is why most
of Prophet Muhammad's Sahabat's graves are away from Mekah
and Madinah as they begin to travel after the passing of Prophet
Muhammad.

In a Hadith by Ibnu Abdil Barr:

To seek for knowledge is <u>Wajib</u> to all Muslim men and Muslim women

The other <u>Ayats</u> that mentions about the importance of travel include the followings: -

Do they not travel through the earth, and see what was the End of those before them (who did evil)? Allah brought utter destruction on them, and similar (fates await) those who reject Allah.
Muhammad 47: 10

Say: "Go ye through the earth and see what has been the end of those guilty (of sin)."
An-Naml 27:69

Many were the Ways of Life that have passed away before you: travel through the earth, and see what was the end of those who rejected Truth.
Ali-Imran 3:137

Seest thou not that the ships sail through the ocean by the Grace of Allah that He may show you of His Signs? Verily in this are Signs for all who constantly persevere and give thanks.
Luqman 31:31

Say: "Travel through the earth and see what was the end of those before (you): Most of them worshipped others besides Allah."
Ar-Rumm 30:42

Do they not travel through the earth, and see what was the end
of those before them? They were superior to them in strength:
they tilled the soil and populated it in greater numbers than
these have done: there came to them their apostles with Clear
(Signs). (Which they rejected, to their own destruction): It was
not Allah Who wronged them, but they wronged their own souls.
Ar-Rumm 30:9

The Quran has clearly mentioned in the Ayats the need to travel,
see the world and learn from all that we can find. It's a good
narration that we can follow to ensure that we learn from the
past mistakes of others and better prepare ourselves to become a
good human being.

Similarly, in the perspective of airports, ports and logistics, we
need to learn few lessons from all the Ayats. Among others is
that we need to prepare the necessities before we travel. For
instance, if a truck is scheduled to be driven over 500 kilometres,
the trucking manager should make preparation to give the truck
driver enough money for his motive power, toll, food allowance
and other needs. The truck too needs to be road-worthy to
endure a 500 kilometres journey. However, if the journey is just
a mere 10 kilometres, the preparation might not be as detail as a
500-kilometre journey.

Secondly, the drivers need to have the knowledge of the journey.
This include the SOP to handle the document and the cargo, SOP
of driving and the SOP to take rest. The drivers too need to know
the location of the delivery.

Next, we need to comply to the local regulations. Trucks need to comply to the police laws, road transport law and Incoterms.

Last but not the least, one of the best practices that we can learn from the Ayats of the Quran is that the Allah created a world is easy to us to travel and to witness His Greatness. We should always be thankful and give back to the needy at all time.

III) Air Transportation

Air transportation is critical enabler to achieving economic growth and development. In the 1970s, the world recorded some 310,441,392 passengers who flew on aircrafts. Fast forward in 2018, we have recorded a massive 4.23 billion people who travel on aircrafts. Similarly, in 1973, the world recorded only 15,568 MT of cargo being flown in aircraft. In 2019, the tonnage has increase to more than 1000%. With more people and cargo being flown across the globe, we can expect more business transaction to materialized.

Air transportation too facilitates integration into the global economy and provides vital connectivity on a national, regional, and international scale. It helps generate promote tourism, international trade and create employment opportunities.

According to US National Safety Council, flying in a commercial airliner is the safest form of transportation. In the analysis done by US Census data, the odds of dying as an aircraft passenger is only 1 in 205,552 people. This is much better that the odd for dying as a cyclist (1 in 4,050), the odds of drowning (1 in 1,986) and in car crash (1 in 102). Air is known for its highest safety

standards and is the highest regulated transportation mode for security.

The stories of the birds can be implied to understand how God allows easy flying of the aircrafts. Can you image how the aircraft which weight thousands MT can fly on air? How is it for the aircraft to stay afloat with such tremendous burden? Of course, some engineering concepts has to be applied. Moreover, Allah said in Surat An-Nahl: -

Do they not look at the birds, held poised in the midst of (the air and) the sky? Nothing holds them up but (the power of) Allah. Verily in this are signs for those who believe.
An-Nahl 16:79

Do *they not observe the birds above them, spreading their wings and folding them in? None can uphold them except ((Allah)) Most Gracious: Truly ((Allah)) Most Gracious: Truly it is He that watches over all things.*
Al-Mulk 67:19

Verily in the heavens and the earth, are Signs for those who believe.
Al-Jaathiyah 45:3

g) Unit load devices

The Quran has 114 Surat with 6,236 Ayats. Although the statistics looks like it's big, but the world has millions of people who a Huffaz. They are able to memorize the Quran with no flaws.

Can you name anyone who can memorize a book line by line, word by work that is about the size of Harry Porters' book "Harry Potter and the Sorcerer's Stone"? There are 76,944 words in the Harry Potter book. Comparatively the are 77,449 words in the Quran. It just about the same size, but there is no way for us to find anyone who can memorize Harry Porter's book line by line.

How God make the Quran easy to memorize? The secret is in "small chunks". Surat Al-Qamar said: -

And We have indeed made the Qur'an easy to understand and remember: then is there any that will receive admonition?
Al-Qamar 54:17,32,40
(repeated 3 times)

But We have indeed made the Qur'an easy to understand and remember: then is there any that will receive admonition?
AL-Qamar 54:22

All the Ayats in the Quran has been preserved for thousands of years. The words that is in the Quran now is the same that has been taught from Jibril to Prophet Muhammad.

The same goes with unit load devices best practices. To be able to have better grasp of the cargo, we need to make it in a palatable way. The portion has to be small but quantifiable. We need to able to record all the cargo movements in and out, identify the location and able to record any flaws to the cargo.

h) Accounting & Record Keeping

Thousands of years ago, history has shown that the Mesopotamians were able to document all the list of expenditure, goods received and goods traded. The record keeping process is admired but it has it flaws as it focused only in the context of controlling goods, stock and transaction for the benefit of the temples in Mesopotamia. At about the same time too, we can also find early accounting records in the ruins of ancient Babylon, Assyria and Sumeria. The people of that time relied on primitive accounting methods to record the growth of crops and herds.

Fast forward, the modern accounting system was said to be founded with the introduction of a double entry system. Goryeo Dynasty (918-1392 CE) of Korea has been credited by historians as the founder of the system. The earliest double entry system in Europe on the other hand came from Amatino Manucci, a Florentine merchant at the end of the 13th century. Manucci was employed by the Farolfi firm and the firm's ledger provided evidences of full double-entry bookkeeping records.

Double entry accounting system has many benefits such as: -

*   ensures the arithmetical accuracy of the books (of accounts).
*   It prevents and minimizes frauds.
*   If there are frauds, the frauds can be detected early.
*   Errors can be checked and rectified easily.
*   This system provides information in decision making.

Many people did not realize that the Quran has shown about the importance of double entry system some 1,400 years ago. In the Quran, there are 23 Ayats that mention about every living creation is created in pairs. Why should they be in pairs? It will check back all the benefits that we have listed a paragraph earlier that is to: -

✓ ensures the arithmetical accuracy of the books.
✓ It prevents and minimizes frauds.
✓ If there are frauds, the frauds can be detected early.
✓ Errors can be checked and rectified easily.
✓ This system provides information in decision making.

Amazing is it? Now let's review some of the Ayats in the Quran that mention about this

Glory to Allah, Who created in pairs all
things that the earth produces,
as well as their own (human) kind
and (other) things of which they have no knowledge.
Yaa Siin 36:36

And Allah did create you from dust; then from a sperm-drop;
then He made you in pairs. And no female conceives, or lays
down (her load), but with His knowledge. Nor is a man long-
lived granted length of days, nor is a part cut off from his
life, but is in a Decree (ordained). All this is easy to Allah.
Al-Faatir 35:11

*(He is) the Creator of the heavens and the earth: He
has made for you pairs from among yourselves, and
pairs among cattle: by this means does He multiply
you: there is nothing whatever like unto Him, and
He is the One that hears and sees (all things).*
Asy-Syuura 42:11

*That has created pairs in all things, and has made
for you ships and cattle on which ye ride,*
Az-Zukhruf 43:12

*And of everything We have created pairs: That
ye may receive instruction to Glorify Allah*
Adz-Dzaariyaat 51:49

In them will be Fruits of every kind, two and two.
Ar-Rahmaan 55:52

And (have We not) created you in pairs,
An-Naba' 78:8

Paul Dirac, a British researcher observed and confirmed that
every material on earth was created in pairs in his theory called
"Antimatter". Although Dirac was initially hesitant about sharing
his findings, but he eventually declared that every particle in the
universe would have a mirror image. A mirror image in this case
can be assumed as "in pairs". Dirac received a Nobel Prize in
Physics in 1933 for this discovery.

There are many other <u>Ayat</u>'s in the Quran that explains objects in pair. For instance: -

- Life and death – were mentioned 145 times
- Good and bad deeds – were mentioned 167 times
- World and afterlife - were mentioned 115 times
- Angel and Satan – were mentioned 88 times
- Man and woman – were mentioned 24 times
- Ill fate and goodness – were mentioned 75 times

And many more.

Even if we study the botany of plants, we began to understand that there are male and female plants. The male plant needs the female plant to breed and bear fruits.

This is an excellent lesson of best practices that we can get from the Quran, that is to record everything in pairs.

Wallahualam!

CHAPTER 5

Risk Management

The concept of managing risks in operations surfaced sometime after World War II when companies began to focus more on operational profit rather that engaging into wars. Modern risk management is said to start after 1955. Operational risk and liquidity risk management emerged in the 1990s. International regulation of risk also began in the 1990s. After 1990s the progress has developed very fast to meet up with the fast-changing world.

Initially, the concept hovers around the application of insurance. Today it has evolved not just insurance but to all aspects of operations including engineering risks, political risks, financial risks, operation risks and accidents risks. Of course, the detail is much deeper. For instance, when we talk about financial risk, we also cover hedging activities, insurance premium risks, exchange rate volatility, customer loan payment risks and many more.

In another instance, airports, ports and logistics too possess many risks especially the operational risk. Huge steps have been taken by operating companies to control these risks. Some of the notable business risks include operational delays, safety risks, security risks, equipment breakdown, human resources management, traffic

conditions, weather conditions and many more. All these if it is not managed well will bring possible financial losses to the airports, ports and logistics companies. The act of self-protection the organization is an important element of risk mitigation. Anticipating problems will reduce the probabilities of losses or unwanted costs before they arise.

The main objective of risk management is to maximize firm value. This can be achieved with the reduction of costs associated with different risks. Some of the major cost elements that companies incur are income taxes, financial distress, project financing and operational inefficiency cost.

The other objective of risk management is to improve the firm's capital structure, which suggests that companies in good financial health should use their information advantage to establish strategies to hedge future prices.

Today risk management is recognized as a major issue of corporate governance. Its main orientations and risk guidelines must be defined by the board of directors. The risks too are commonly be monitored by independent, competent directors in the audit committee or the risk management committee.

The Quran has long recognized the importance of risk management. However, the concept was not detail out to make the content relevant across centuries, countries and cultures. Below is the Ayat that should be the basis of foundation of risk management in Islam.

Indeed, Allah [alone] has knowledge of the Hour and sends down the rain and knows what is in the wombs. And no soul

perceives what it will earn tomorrow, and no soul perceives in *what land it will die. Indeed, Allah is Knowing and Acquainted*
Luqman 31:34

In the Ayat, the Quran has warned us that we do not know what will happen in the future. We would not know how many profits can we get and we should not know to when and where we will die. Being young now does not promise that you will live long, as only Allah knows when you will die. We have been warned ahead to be prepared at all time.

There is another Hadith that reminds us to be prepared at all time. Of course, we need to continuous submit and Tawakkal to Allah, but at the same time too we need to plan so that no mishaps or losses can happen due to our own carelessness or laziness.

Anas ibn Malik reported:

A man said, "O Messenger of Allah, should I tie my *camel and trust in Allah, or should I leave her untied* *and trust in Allah?" The Prophet, peace and blessings* *be upon him, said, "Tie her and trust in Allah."*
Source: Sahih Al-Tirmidhi

In another Ayat as shown below, the Quran reminded us again about the importance to plan ahead for tomorrow. There is no certainty of what we have planned will be successful because Allah knows what is best for all. But we need to get prepared because it is our responsibility to be the servant of Allah.

O you who have believed, fear Allah. And let every soul
look to what it has put forth for tomorrow - and fear
Allah. Indeed, Allah is Acquainted with what you do.
Al-Hashar 59:18

The concept of managing the uncertainty is the main element to Islamic risk management. Naturally, no one with a sound mind would be investing and expecting losses. Even at the macro level, leaders of the countries will evaluate projects and will push for positive growth. The ability to produce sound risk management system will then allow the prudent growth of the country.

And spend in the way of Allah and <u>do not throw [yourselves]</u>
<u>*with your [own] hands into destruction [by refraining].*</u>
And do good; indeed, Allah loves the doers of good
Al-Baqarah 1:195

This chapter about Risk Management too is not complete unless we requote back the story of strategic planning by Prophet Yusof which we have mentioned earlier. The story has been mentioned from Ayat 46-49.

Yusof, O man of truth, explain to us about seven fat cows
eaten by seven [that were] lean, and seven green spikes
[of grain] and others [that were] dry - that I may return
to the people; perhaps they will know [about you]."

Yusof said, "You will plant for seven years
consecutively; and what you harvest leave in its
spikes, except a little from which you will eat.

Then will come after that seven difficult [years]
which will consume what you saved for them,
except a little from which you will store

Then will come after that a year in which the people will be
given rain and in which they will press [olives and grapes].
Yusof 12:46-49

In these Ayats, the Quran has advised us the importance of risk management. In fact, if we look into most world economic patterns, we can detect its ups and down cycles.

The economic cycle or business cycle, can be categorized into four main classification that is expansion, peak, contraction and trough. During the expansion phase, the economy experiences relatively rapid growth, interest rates tend to be low, production increases, and inflationary pressures build. But do remember that a prolonged expansion phrase will create a heating economy.

After a while the overheating economy needs to cools down and that actually creates a down cycle. From the year 1945 to the year 2014, the National Bureau of Economic Research (NBER) defined twelve cycles, with the average cycle lasting about 6 years. This is very close to the advice given in Surat Yusof above where we were told to be aware about the seven-year cycle!

That why we need to mitigate the risks by being prudent.

Wallahualam!

CHAPTER 6

KPI in Quran

Key Performance Indicators or better known as KPI, is the main yardstick to measure airports, ports and logistics performance. All good organizations have set up the KPI for the organization, the department and also individual. Failing to meet the KPI normally translate to bad work performance. KPIs are measures that help you understand whether you are achieving one or more of your strategic goals.

KPI too is closely related to performance bonus and also promotions. Thus, every employee tries as much possible to achieve the targets given to them. But, how does KPI relates to Islamic teachings? Do you really need KPI in your organization? Let us first try to determine a KPI. We like to recommended just six steps that will guide you to set up a great KPI: -

Step	Actions Required
1	Get very clear direction about what a KPI or performance that you want to measure
2	Evaluate your existing KPI and performance measures to decide what to keep, what to enhance and what to eliminate

3	Use the SMART Principles to create a KPI
	S – Smart
	M – measurable
	A – Achievable
	R – Realistic
	T – Timely
4	Make sure your goals are measurable before you develop performance measurement.
5	Set the realistic goals
6	Before the KPI has been firmed up, get the buy-in among the people who you need to support the KPIs.

Table 2: *6 Steps to Great KPI*

Is there any mention of about KPI in the Quran? In the Surat Al-Baqarah, Allah has mentioned that: -

Allah does not charge a soul except with that within its
capacity. It will have what good it has gained, and it will
bear what evil it has earned. "Our Lord, do not impose
blame upon us if we have forgotten or erred. Our Lord,
and lay not upon us a burden like that which You laid
upon those before us. Our Lord, and burden us not with
that which we have no ability to bear. And pardon us;
and forgive us; and have mercy upon us. You are our
protector, so give us victory over the disbelieving people
Al-Baqarah 2:286

The above Ayat recommends that the SMART principle is to be used to set up proper KPI to all airports, ports and logistics

operations. *Within its capacity* means that Allah asks us to do something that is "realistic".

For instance, if we force drivers to deliver goods to 25 locations within 8 hours, but the traffic condition is really bad and the distance is too far away, while the normal delivery will take 12 hours. Forcing the drivers to perform beyond their means will possibly create robust drivers, "I don't care drivers", dangerous drivers, drivers who don't eat proper meals and possibly drivers who forgo their daily prayers. It is not proper to force drivers to perform beyond their means.

In a Hadith from Abu Hurairah as narrated by Muslim, the Prophet Muhammad SAW said: -

> *Allah will not force anyone from a deed unless*
> *the deed is something that he is able to do,*

KPI is actually a guideline to achieve the goals of a work that has been entrusted to a worker. Thus, is it a sin if a worker did not achieve his or her KPI? This is a very interesting question but Allah has given us the answer in the Quran. To answer this, we will review two scenarios: -

Scenario 1: If the KPI is not fulfilled because of laziness or work without enthusiasm, the workers are deemed not to fulfil his or her entrusted responsibilities. This is clearly stated in the Quran: -

> *O you who have believed, do not betray Allah*
> *and the Messenger or betray your trusts*
> *while you know [the consequence]*
> **Al-Anfal 8:27**

The instruction has been clearly given in the Quran, thus the act of not fulfilling her or her KPI because of laziness may be a sinful act.

Scenario 2: If the KPI is not fulfilled because the job is beyond the worker capacity, it may not be a sinful act. We have quoted this earlier in this chapter whereby it was mentioned that

> *Allah does not charge a soul except with that within its capacity ... (until end).*
> **Al-Baqarah 2:286**

A true KPI for a Muslim is actually his level of Takwa to Allah.

> *O mankind, indeed We have created you from male and female and made you peoples and tribes that you may know one another. Indeed, the most noble of you in the sight of Allah is the most righteous of you. Indeed, Allah is Knowing and Acquainted*
> **Al-Hujurat 49:13**

Takwa comes from the word *Waqa, Yaqi* and *Wiqatayan* which means protection. Takwa is actually to protect own self from all the evil and improper things that is prohibited by Allah. Takwa also means to adhere to the instructions that has been given by Allah.

Wallahualam!

CHAPTER 7

Other important elements

In addition to the best practises presented earlier, there are many other elements that airports, ports and logistics professionals needs to be guided from the Quran. Among others are issues like safety, security and environment. The Quran, has long emphasize these three elements in our daily life's. Unfortunately, the greed of mankind supersedes the importance of these elements.

Thus, we saw for many years people has been working in a very bad working conditions that their health conditions worsen. For instance, the United States *Occupational Safety and Health Administration Act* was only established in 1971. Before that, there is no act whatsoever that looks into the safety wellbeing of the workers. Upon establishment of an act, then only we are able to see dramatic effect of workplace safety. It was reported that there were some 14,000 workers were killed on the job in 1970. Comparatively the number dropped to only 4,340 workers in 2009. Please note too that the U.S. employment was a high 130 million workers from more than 7 million worksite. Since the passage of the OSH Act, the rate of reported serious workplace injuries and illnesses has declined from 11 per 100 workers in 1972 to 3.6 per 100 workers in 2009.

In another example, the *Occupational Safety and Health Act* in Malaysia was only established 1994; while the revised *Workplace Safety and Health Act* is issued by the Republic of Singapore only in 2006. Can you imagine the workers condition before the establishment of the act?

a)   Safety & Security

The importance of safety in airports, ports and logistics operations has become very critical today. This comes with the continues education and upskilling of the workforce. In this book, we combine together safety and security in one section as it is closely related. Interestingly, both of the words peace and security has been combined in 2 of the Ayats.

(Their greeting will be): "Enter ye here in peace and security.
Al-Hijr 15:46

There can they call for every kind of fruit in peace and security
Ad-Dukhan 44:55

There is no other religion in this world that calls for peace like Islam. To start with, the greetings of Muslims too starts with "peace". Assalamualaikum generally means 'peace be unto you' or, 'peace be with you'. End the end of every Solat, it is Wajib to utter the greetings of Assalamulaikum too. More often paradise is called the "abode of peace" where there the dwellers will stay in the paradise forever and speaks only peaceful words.

Islam has never submitted to humiliation and aggression. Thus, when Islam talks about the permission for Jihad against the

enemies of Islam, it actually means as self-defence and while resisting occupation. Once the occupation came to an end and aggression stopped, it would eventually bring peace and safeguard others' rights. The ethic of war in Islam is simple – as self-defence. As state in few Ayats: -

Fight in the way of Allah against those who fight
against you, but begin not hostilities
Al-Baqarah 2:190

There should be no hostility except against the oppressors
Al-Baqarah 2:193

Islam dictates that Muslims are to make peace with their enemy. If the enemy has stopped its aggression and move to incline peace, then all of us should revert back to peace. As stated in the Quran: -

And if they incline to peace, incline thou also to it, and
trust in Allah. Lo! He is the Hearer, the Knower
Al-Anfal 8:61

As explained earlier, Islam clearly dictates that fighting is legislated only as a mean for defending the rights of the oppressed. Terrorism is never part of Islamic preaching's. Thus, the whole media propaganda for Islam as a violent religion is not correct. The Islamophobia phenomenon was created to instil hate towards the peaceful religion of Islam.

And why should ye not fight in the cause of Allah and of
those who, being weak, are ill treated (and oppressed)?
Whose cry is: Our Lord rescue us from this town whose

people are oppressors; and raise for us from thee one who
will protect; and raise for us from thee one who will help.
Those who believe fight in the cause of Allah, and those who
reject Faith fight in the cause of evil: so, fight ye against the
friends of Satan: feeble indeed is the cunning of Satan
An-Nisaa' 4:75-76

Based on the above, it becomes clear that Islam is the religion of peace and safety, and there is no room therein for violence or aggression.

The same goes with the airports, ports and logistics security aspect. As much as we like peace, we also value the security that we can have. The security from theft, the security from frustration, the security of monetary freedom and of course the security from hell fire. After all, the word security has been mentioned 16 times in the Quran.

Do ye feel secure that He Who is in heaven will not cause
you to be swallowed up by the earth when it shakes (as in an
earthquake)? Or do ye feel secure that He Who is in Heaven
will not send against you a violent tornado (with showers of
stones), so that ye shall know how (terrible) was My warning?
Al-Mulk 67:16 & 17

People needs security from the unwanted things just like the airports, ports and logistics practices. Cargo owners needs the cargo to have the highest number of security possible from all area and from all possible scenarios. Unsecured cargo means that

there are possibilities for defects and possible losses. This should not be a criterion in handling efficient operations.

Furthermore, security in airports, ports and logistics industry means that we need to ensure that the customers feel safe doing business with us. They should be allowed to sleep peacefully knowing that their cargo is in good hands.

Will ye be left secure, in (the enjoyment
of) all that ye have here?
Ash-Shuara 26:146

It is our duty to ensure that safety and security factors of the cargo is at the highest standards. As Allah has shown us His gracefulness and kindness to mankind, we should also be grateful and repay back to the highest level of appreciation. The only way to return this favour is by doing the great airports, ports and logistics operation jobs that satisfy the 7 R's of logistics and able to delight the customers.

## b)	Environment

Another area that was previously neglected was the environment issues. God has created earth with so much detail that it impossible for man to replicate a simple life form. In 2019, it was estimated that there are more than 7.5 billion living humans in this planet. And that represents more than 7.5 billion different thumbprints for mankind. Can you imagine how perfect Allah has created human being to be the same but so different individually.

The world was originally full of vegetations and freshness. That's the same original condition that we can expect to experience in the gardens of paradise. Fascinatingly, the Quran has lots of stories about the greens in the paradise. There are more than ten types of fruits and vegetations that is mentioned in the Quran including dates, bananas, grapes, pomegranate, garlic, herbs, ginger, olives, lentils, onion, cucumber, figs, mustard, and some variety of trees including the cedar and the acacia flower.

There are 41 Ayats in the Quran that mentions about eating fruits including: -

They will recline on Carpets, whose inner linings will be of rich brocade: the Fruit of the Gardens will be near (and easy of reach).
Ar-Rahman, 54

Among Talh trees with flowers (or fruits) piled one above another
Al-Waqiah, 29

The Fruits whereof (will hang in bunches) low and near.
Al-Haqqa, 23

And (they shall have) fruits, all they desire.
Al-Mursalat, 42

What can we learn from this? Fruits and grains are already part of our diet. The Quran allows eating Halal meat from cows, goat, birds, fish etc. However, there is no mentioned about which one is better.

But the Quran did mention to eat a balanced diet. The benefits of fruits as good nourishment can be understood from this verse which cover the whole range of fruits, salads, and vegetables which also play an important role in a nutritious, balanced diet:

It is He who sends down rain from the sky, and with it. We bring forth vegetation of all kinds, and out of it We bring forth thick clustered grain. And out of the date palm and its spate come clusters of dates hanging low and near, and gardens of grapes, olives and pomegranates each similar (in kind) yet different (in variety and taste). Look at their fruits when then begin to bear, and the ripeness thereof.

Al-Anam 6:99

Islam, being a complete religion, also teaches and advises the believer as to what the best method of eating is. The believers are advised to be moderate in every aspect of life. Direct reference has been made in the Noble Quran regarding moderation in eating and drinking.

And eat and drink, but waste not in extravagance, certainly He (Allah) likes not those who waste in extravagance

Al-A'raf 7:31

What can we further learn here from this Ayats? These can be some reminder to us that we should be thinking about how to continuously green the earth. Mankind has been considered as the major factor is environmental disruption. Trees are cut, mountains are levelled, waste are produced, air is polluted thus interfering the natural balances of earth ecosystem.

Mankind has created irreversible pollution in our water, air and land. The causes of the pollutions vary. We will discuss the pollutions here in the perspective of transport industry: -

i) Air Pollution

The air pollution is expected to happen with the usage of motored vehicles. All vehicles use motive power. The main method to generate the motive power has always been fossil fuel like petrol, diesel and coal. Unfortunately, fossil fuel produces negative combustion to the atmosphere especially carbon dioxide. Other contaminants like nitrogen oxides, hydrocarbon too is unceremoniously produced.

ii) Noise Pollution

The second type of pollution that is very disturbing is the noise pollution. Noise is distracting and irritating. Have you been camping in a forest and hear nothing except the sounds of crickets and flowing river? Can you compare the scenario while sleeping in a house which is adjacent to the main road?

The main source of noise pollution comes from motor vehicles. The noise is measured in "decibel" (dB) or "phon", the former being the unit of sound pitch, the latter being the unit of its pressure or impact. However, decibel is more commonly used. The lower the decibels are more acceptable. Continuous exposure to noises of more than 100 decibel is damaging to human ears.

140	Threshold of Pain
130	Jet Taking Off (60 meters away)
120	Operating Heavy Equipment
110	Night Club with Loud Music
100	Construction Site
90	Boiler Room
80	Freight Train (30 meters away)
70	Classroom Chatter
60	Conversation (1 meter away)
50	Urban Residence
40	Soft Whisper (1.5 meter away)
30	North Rim of Grand Canyon
20	Silent Study Room
10	
0	Threshold of Hearing (1,000 Hz)

Figure 2

Typical Sound Levels (dBA)

There are <u>Ayat</u>s that call to avoid noise, such as the following:

*Neither speak thy prayer aloud, nor speak it in a
low tone, but seek a middle course between.*
Al-Israa 17:110

*O you who believe, raise not your voices above the voice
of the Prophet. Nor speak aloud to him in talk, as you may
speak aloud to one another, lest your deeds become void
and you perceive not. Those that lower their voices in the
presence of the apostle of Allah – their hearts have Allah
tested for piety: for them is forgiveness and a great Reward.*
Al-Hujurat: 2:3

iii) Water Pollution

Years ago, people can just take the river water and drink from it. Today, water has to be treated first with using very advanced and expensive machines to purify the water. Why is this so? Didn't Allah create clean rivers?

Transportation is one of the sources of water pollution. The other source of water pollution comes from the construction and maintenance of the roads, railway and ports. Realizing the need, the are many international laws that has been govern to control various pollutions. *Marine Pollution (MARPOL) Act* from the *International Maritime Organization (IMO)* has produced a strict guideline for ships to adhere including factors like control of oil originating from ballast tank arrangements, limits of sulphur oxide from ship exhaust emissions, controlling sewage disposal and many more.

All types of pollutions are further enhanced with urbanization of the populations, especially when it is close to more natural resources. The urbanization actually disturbs the existing natural balance of the ecosystem. This imbalance is mainly attributed to the increasing disposal of human waste, industrial waste, exploitation of resources and density in population. This irresponsible behaviour has led to a depletion in the atmosphere and this produces the greatest threat worldwide. Moreover, mankind has created more waste than ever. Even disturbingly is the plastic waste that is not degradable for hundreds of years.

Some major effect of the pollutions includes the depletion of the ozone layer, the global warming, the melting of the ice at the north

and south pole, the removal of the forest, the extinction of wild animals, the widening of the deserts and many more. One thing leads to another and the whole eco-system is disrupted.

The ozone layer too has been proven to be depleting. Thanks to the exhaust of the flying aircrafts in the higher altitude and also the release of chlorofluorocarbons gases, halons and freons worldwide since the 1970's. Although these gases have been banned, but the increase thinning meaning that earth is losing its protective layer. As Quran is a book of science, it did mention about the protecting of the atmosphere.

And We made the sky a protected ceiling (canopy),
but they, from its signs, are turning away."
Al-Anbya 21:32

It is Allah who made for you the earth a place of settlement
and the sky a ceiling and formed you and perfected your
forms and provided you with good things. That is Allah,
your Lord; then blessed is Allah, Lord of the worlds
Ghafir 40:64

Is it a miracle that the Quran already mentioned about this some 1,400 years ago. Prophet Muhammad would not have made it up. The knowledge of atmosphere only came to the scientist's knowledge in the late 1960s. Allah too has specifically mentioned in the Quran that He loves not those who spread mischiefs.

There is the type of man whose speech about this world's
life may dazzle thee, and he calls The God (Allah) to

witness about what is in his heart: yet is he the most
contentious of enemies? When he turns his back, his aim
everywhere is to spread mischief through the earth and
destroy crops and cattle. But Allah loves not mischief
Al-Baqarah 1: 204 & 205

Mischief has appeared on the land and sea, because
of (the need) that the hands of man have earned, that
(Allah) may give them a taste of some of their deeds:
in order that they may turn back (from evil)
Ar-Rum 30:41

As conclusion, all airports, ports and logistics practitioners should always be thinking on methods to improve operations and reduces the pollution. Allah only loans to mankind this earth in order for mankind to continue benefiting the universe. Unfortunately, mankind disrupts the balance and created more damages than goods.

Business and economic development is needed for the growth of a nation. But at the same time too, all logisticians need to plan for the sustainability of the earth. Our children depend on all us for the own survival.

The Quran tells the story of how the perfect milieu should be like in the paradise. The paradise is referred as green, serene, happy place and peaceful. That is what all logistics operations should work for.

And it is He (God) who has made you successors (Khalifa)
upon the earth and has raised some of you above
others in degrees [of rank] that He may try you through
what He has given you. Indeed, your Lord is swift in
penalty; but indeed, He is Forgiving and Merciful
Al-An'am 6:165

Gone were the days of dirty unorganized warehouse. We should be thinking on how to move forward towards creating Green Airports, Green Ports and Green Logistics. After all, the Quran is actually the ultimate Green Book Policy.

Were all of mankind to come together and wish to
produce the like of the Qur'an, they would never
succeed, however much they aided each other.
Al-Israaq 17:88

Wallahualam!

CHAPTER 8

Scholars view about Quran

The Quran is the words of Allah that was first handed down to Prophet Muhamad not as a book, but just verbal revelation. Over the years, the Sahabat has worked together to write so that it will be preserved. As promised by Allah, all the writings were able to be collected and the integrity of the Quran has never been compromised.

> *Verily, We have made this (Qur'an) easy, in thy*
> *tongue, in order that they may give heed.*
> **Ad-Dukhan 44:58**

We managed to compile few statements from our Islamic scholars about the Quran. The list is not exhaustive as there are many other views about the Quran:-

a) Imam Muslim

> *"The Quran is the medicine to all type of sickness except death. May Allah grant all of us with Iman, and to return back to Him in Iman with our lips still wet to recite the sacred Ayats of the Quran"*

b) Imam Syafie

> *"Anyone who talks based on Quran and Sunnah is the correct one. Other than that, the deeds look to be of a waste"*

c) Al-Harith Al-Muhasibi

> *"For those who reads the Quran to get its <u>Pahala</u>, you might as well look for the examples and the stories from the Quran"*

d) Fudhail bin Iyadh

> *"The keeper of the Quran will be able to prevent the anger of Allah. How can they make sins when the words of Quran pray for him "Dear Allah, please do not allow he/she to do what you don't want he/she to do it"*

e) Abdul Qadir al-Jilaini

> *"O yee my tribe. Please be good to the Quran by following its words and not to dispute/argue with it"*

f) Imam Ibn Taimiyyah

> *"The Quran will cure all diseases that cause you to have evil desires, until your soul has been cleaned and you return back to your original state (fitrah). Then you become purified"*

g) Ibn Qayyim

> *"The Quran is the words of Allah"*

h) Mustafa Al-Sibai

> *"The Quran will touch the hearts of people to reads and follow it. Hearing the Quran recitals from the radio will open up your heart towards iman; this is much better that 1,000 other programs"*

i) Dr Yusof Al-Qaradhawi

> *"Mentioned that the Quran is the way of life to human being. He also mentioned that for whoever is at loss, we must refer back to the Quran as is the main source of law and dakwah"*

Being able to read and interpret the stories in the Quran is expected to make readers a better human being. The Quran is the most complete and universal law book whose knowledge covers all aspects of life and business.

The ability to narrate the stories and words of Allah in the Quran, and relate it to the business world will ensure business survival as Allah will be reward the faithful follower with the ultimate win – the Jannah.

There are evidence of airports, ports and logistics knowledge in the Quran. This book has shown it although readers have to narrate it with the actual logistics process. Thus, it is up to the airports, ports and the logisticians to follow the examples of the best practices.

Wallahualam!

Closure

There are many things in life that we can find in the Quran. Stories, life, love, peace, scientific knowledge, geography, astronomy, laws and many others. The Quran is the word of Allah that has been revealed to Prophet Muhammad to this universe. The Quran is a real miracle.

Airports, ports and logistics knowledge too can be found in the Quran as has been revealed in this book. It is not directly dictated but can be digested via implied narratives. We should extract it out and then analyse to fit to the industry.

May this book continue to benefit the majority of the all logistics practitioners of the world because this book is not just confined to Muslims. God willing, I pray that the non-Muslims will one day find the Hidayah that all of us are looking for. I pray too that Prophet Muhammad will look into this effort of the writer and also the readers with Redha, as a source for him to provide us with the much needed Shafaat during the judgement day, Insyallah.

Do spread the word about this book to the others. Hopefully, all of us can gain some Pahala from Allah. As reported in a Hadith Sahih: -

Abu Huraira reported: The Messenger of Allah, peace and blessings be upon him, said, "When the human being dies, his deeds end except for three: ongoing charity, beneficial knowledge, or a righteous child who prays for him."

Source: Sahih Muslim

There are also other areas in logistics operations that that was not mentioned but we need to study like Halal logistics and Halal procurement. These two areas are also implied in the narratives of the Quran. The knowledge of the Quran is indeed unlimited.

This book is the world first analysis of the best practices at airports, ports and logistics as extracted out from the Quran. I have taken a lot of effort to ensure the accuracy of the information. However, if there are any mistakes, it is from my own inefficiency.

The Quran is indeed an Ajaba.

The Quran is perfect right from the beginning.

Wallahualam!

References and Further Readings

Al-Quran

Bichou, K. (2009). Port Operations, Planning & Logistics. Informa Law

Daily Hadith Online, https://abuaminaelias.com/dailyhadithonline/

Field, P. (2003). Introduction to Modern Risk Management, A History, London: Incisive RWG, Haymarket House

Henio, E. (1992) "Accounting Numbers as 'inscription': Action at a Distance and the Development of Accounting." *Accounting, Organizations and Society* 17 (7): 685–708

Quran Index, https://www.quranindex.net/

Shamsudin, N. and Sham, R. (2016). Fundamentals of Transport. Oxford University Press

The Noble Quran, https://quran.com/

The Muslim Village, https://muslimvillage.com/

UNCTAD (1985). Port Development Handbook, United Nations.

UNCTAD (2017). Port Performance Indicators, United Nations.

World Bank Data. https://data.worldbank.org/indicator/

Yahya, Nazry (2016). Fundamentals of Operational Logistics. Oxford University Press

Yahya, Nazry (2018). Fundamentals of Operational Logistics, Asian Edition. Oxford University Press

Wallahualam!

Glossary

Ajaba	The Miracles
Amanah	Trust. Devotion. Guardianship. Loyalty
Amal Makruf	The concept of doing good deeds
Assalamualaikum	Peace be with you
Ayat	Is the verses in a Surat
Buraq	Vehicle the prophet uses during Israq Mikraj
Doa	Pray and hope to Allah
Gharar	Unclear status whether of halal or haram
Hadith	The quoted words of Prophet Muhammad
Halal	Permissible. Allowable
Haram	Not permissible. It's a No.
Hidayah	The show of correct path from Allah
Huffaz	People who memorize the Quran by heart
Husnu Zon	Good thought or intentions
Iqrak	Read
Jannah	Paradise.
Jin	An invisible entity that Allah created
Lillahi Taala	We work because of Allah
Muhasabah	Check with own self
Mukjizat	The miracles of prophets
Nahi Mungkar	The concept of no sins
Niat	Intentions (whether good or bad)
Pahala	Good deeds as recorded by the Angel Raqib
Qasas	Stories. Narratives

Rahmat	Mercy
RA	Rahmatullah
Redha	Pure acceptance
Rezeki	God's gift
Sahabat	Friends of the Prophet Muhamad SAW
Sahih	Authentic
SAW	Sallahu Alaihi Wassalam
Shahawaat	The evil passion
Shafaat	The help from Prophet Muhammad
Shubuhaat	Doubt
Solat	Prayers
SWT	Subhanahu Wa Taala
Surat	A Surat is the term for a chapter of the Quran
Tafsir	Interpretations of the Quran
Takwa	Level of Iman
Tawakkal	Submission to Allah for help
Ummi	Illiterate
Ustaz	Authorized Islamic teacher
Wajib	Mandatory to do; or it will not be accepted
Zakat	Tilth to enhance the economic standards

Wallahualam!

Surat

Quoted according to sequence

Al-'Alaq	96:1-5
Yusuf	12:111
Al-Qamar	54:17
Ar-Rahman	17:5
Ar-Rahman	17:13,16,18,21,23,25,28,30,32,34,3
	6,38,40,42,45,47,49,51,53,55,57,59,
	61,63,65,67,69,71,73,75,77
	(repeated 31 times)
Aj-Jin	72:1
Al-Kahfi	18:9
Al-Hashar	59:18
Hud	11:56
Az-Zumar	39:21
Al-Baqarah	2:2
Al-Hijr	15: 9
Al-Baqarah	2:282
Al-Baqarah	2:284
Al-Maidah	5:2
An-Nisa	4:58
Al-Anfal	8:27
Al-Mukminum	23:8
Al-Ahzab	33:72
Hud	11:1

Yusof	12:46-49
Al-Asr	103: 1-3
Al-Baqarah	2: 20
Adz-Dzaariyaat	51:49
Az-Zukhruf	43:12
Al-Baqarah	2:23
Al-Baqarah	2:188
Al-Maidah	5:3
Al-Araf	7:33
Al-Mumtahanah	60:8
Hud	11:115
An-Naml	27:17
An-Naml	27: 20
Al-Hajj	22:27
Ar-Rahmaan	55:24
Ibrahim	14:32
Al-Baqarah	2:164
Ghaafir	40:80
Ar-Ruum	30:46
Ibrahim	14:32
Muhammad	47: 10
An-Naml	27:69
Ali-Imran	3:137
Ar-Rumm	30: 42
Luqman	31: 31
Ar-Rumm	30:9
An-Nahl	16:79
Al-Mulk	67:19
Al-Jaathiyah	45:3
Al-Qamar	54: 17,32,40 *(repeated 3 times)*
Al-Qamar	54: 22
Yaa Siin	36:36

Al-Faatir	35:11
Asy-Syuura	42:11
Az-Zukhruf	43:12
Adz-Dzaariyaat	51:49
Ar-Rahmaan	55:52
An-Naba'	78:8
Luqman	31:34
Al-Hashar	59:18
Al-Baqarah	1:195
Yusof	12:46-49
Al-Baqarah	2:286
Al-Anfal	8:27
Al-Baqarah	2:286
Al-Hujurat	49:13
Al-Hijr	15:46
Ad-Dukhan	44:55
Al-Baqarah	2:190
Al-Baqarah	2:193
Al-Anfal	8:61
An-Nisaa'	4:75-76
Al-Mulk	67:16-17
Ash-Shuara	26:146
Ar-Rahman	55:54
Al-Waqiah	56:29
Al-Haqqa	69:23
Al-Mursalat	77:42
Al-Anam	6:99
Al-A'raf	7:31
Al-Israa	17:110
Al-Hujurat	2:3
Al-Anbya	21:32
Ghafir	40:64

Al-Baqarah	2:204-205
Ar-Rum	30:41
Al-An'am	6:165
Al-Israaq	17:88
Ad-Dukhan	44:58

Wallahualam!

The Author

Nazry bin Yahya

Nazry is an expert in airports, ports and logistics operations. He has extensive experience working in the USA, Hong Kong, Malaysia and Vietnam. He is one of the most sought-after speakers at maritime and logistics conferences across Asia. He also trains and lectures at private universities in Malaysia and Vietnam. Nazry is the approved UNCTAD port trainers who is authorized to conduct the prestigious TrainForTrade Port Management Program at all the English-speaking network including countries like Ireland, Croatia, Tanzania, Ghana, Nigeria, Indonesia, Maldives, the Philippines and many others.

Nazry holds a PhD in Commerce from Finders University, Master in Business Administration from Charles Sturt University and a Bachelor degree in Finance from the Eller College, University of Arizona. He is also a Professional Technologist in Transport and Logistics Field (Malaysia Board of Technologist), Chartered Member of CILT, a Registered Fund Manager (Securities Commission of Malaysia), Licensed TPS Manager and a Licensed NLP Practitioner.

He has won numerous world awards including Excellence in Port and Terminal Training (Global Port Forum), Directors Award (FedEx) and also Best Freight Operator (SPAD Malaysia)

Airports, Ports and Logistics Best Practices Discoveries
The Narrative Adaptation from the Quran

www.ingramcontent.com/pod-product-compliance
Lightning Source LLC
Chambersburg PA
CBHW020901310526
45786CB00018B/1081